ESSENTIAL
Practical
WISDOM

For

SENIORS

Spending solutions that don't break the bank

LIN COLLIER

℞REILLOC

ISBN-978-0-9916546-0-4 (Book)
ISBN-978-0-9916546-1-1 (Kindle)

DEDICATION

This book is dedicated to all of the older Americans who we trust are enjoying the fruits of their labor and who wish to continue to do so.

I also dedicate this book to our seven children, eighteen grandchildren and one great grandchild who will hopefully refer to this book for any applicable information in the years to come when they also reach the milestone of senior life.

CONTENTS

ACKNOWLEDGMENTS

Thank you Lord for your guidance, your wisdom, and love!

I would like to thank everyone at Reilloc Publishing, particularly my dear husband Dr. J. Edward Collier, whose teachings on Essential Practical Wisdom have been life transforming.

I thank my amazing family and friends, who provide a caring and attentive support system. Thank you especially to my friend, Pam Pertillar, a mentor and editor. To my high energy aerobic buddies for all their encouragement. And, lastly, I thank all of you who will read this book. I pray that it becomes a best friend, that it changes your life and that your spending habits are impacted for the better. I also hope you pay forward the knowledge obtained as you share it with others.

INTRODUCTION

D oes it ever feel like there is a conspiracy to get your money? If you have, then join the club because seniors are often the prey of predatory business practices and everywhere you turn there is news about a new scam aimed at senior citizens.

Essential Practical Wisdom for Seniors: Spending That Doesn't Break the Bank is the first in a series of books being offered to help senior citizens avoid being financially exploited, which will allow them to enjoy the financial peace that comes with wise spending habits in their remaining years.

Essential Practical Wisdom is a learned behavior where you know to do the right thing at the right time and you do it. Doing the right thing at the right time is basically very good decision making that flows from an intuitive aspect in your life. Someone once said that wisdom is when the actions you take today prove to be the right actions later.

Essential Practical Wisdom for everyday living relates to right action that comes from right thinking. A person can know what to do and not do it, but a wise practical person will act intentionally always endeavoring to do the right thing at the right time.

One of my favorite books we gifted to new parents is titled, *Parenting Isn't for Cowards* by Dr. James Dobson, Founder and Chairman Emeritus of Focus on the Family. Recently I heard someone else make a similar reference to the fact that embracing your role as a senior citizen also isn't for cowards. Immediately, I felt this was a very appropriate way to introduce this book as a valuable tool to help you, the members of your family and your close friends face the challenges inherent in senior living and in fulfilling your purpose. We hope the information you find within these pages proves to be useful and informative and we thank you for purchasing a copy.

We welcome your feedback and invite you to send us your comments concerning this guide. Thank you in advance for your feedback.

Just as important, this book is our way of thanking you for having contributed so much in service to your families and neighborhoods. We hope this guide serves you well.

Lin Collier

SECTION I

ESSENTIAL PRACTICAL WISDOM IN YOUR HOME

CHAPTER 1

BUDGET! BUDGET! BUDGET!

Did you know that seventy percent of the wealth in the United States of America is in the hands of senior citizens? However, the financial exploitation of older people is estimated to cost at least 2.9 billion dollars annually - exploitations that result in substantial loss to senior citizens of their funds, property, and resources.

Your biggest wealth-building tool is the money you receive, whether it's your income, retirement benefits, savings, pensions, or social security. So, it stands to reason that one of the most practical ways to harness the power of your money is by adopting the habit of completing and abiding by a monthly budget (to download a free budget sheet, visit www.essentialpracticalwisdom.com/budget).

The number #1 daily thought of one in every four Americans is money. This can very easily explain why budgeting is such a challenge for most people in our society. In fact, a survey conducted by GO Banking Rates Life + Money revealed that Baby Boomers age 55 to 64 spend 24% of each day thinking about money. Seniors age 65+ spend 18% of each day with money on the brain, with the highest percent of people (32%) thinking about how health and fitness affects their income. These constant thoughts about money might be attributed to credit card debt and retirement savings deficits which are real challenges in a time of life when many seniors are having to survive on a fixed income.

Be encouraged though! You're never too young or too old to start living on a budget. In fact, the peace of mind, stress-relieving freedom, and liberty that comes from living on a budget that helps you tell every single dollar of your fixed income where you want it to go is crucial in your senior years. Stewardship of your finances is a great way to make your income work for you by helping you get out of debt, save for emergencies, invest and pay off your mortgage. Remember: **Doing nothing is not a solution for financial woes**. Even if you're married, living on a stress-relieving budget can make a huge difference in your relationship. Now is the time to make the critical decision to not be driven to the point of no return because one or both of you have overspent your way into serious trouble.

CHAPTER 2

BEWARE! BEWARE! BEWARE

Be alert! You may be at risk for financial exploitation if:

1) You are a senior citizen age 65+, in particular between 80 and 89 years of age.

2) A woman because a scammer thinks a) she's older; b) she's a female, and c) she's unable to protect herself.

3) You are experiencing forgetfulness due to a decline in your cognitive capacity.

4) You live alone, are isolated from your community, have limited social relationships, and you rely on others for your care.

WHAT IS A SCAM? AND HOW DO YOU PROTECT YOURSELF FROM THEM?

Scams are fraudulent schemes or tricks that take advantage of peoples' vulnerabilities, and they are prevalent among those in their senior years.

One way to avoid becoming a scammer's victim is to remember that scams have some distinctive characteristics in common:

1) Scams have "hooks". These "hooks" (such as get-rich-quick schemes and an attitude of entitlement like getting something for nothing, etc.) make scams very attractive to many and focuses too much attention on their attractiveness which causes people to pay too little attention to the red flags that should go up.

2) Scams and scammers are good at charismatic manipulation, and that charisma makes it much easier for you and others to trust the scammers and their "deals."

3) Scammers often approach you with such a sense of urgency that it leaves you little time to make up your mind, while at the same time, making you feel like you'll miss a great opportunity if you don't "act now."

COMMON TYPES OF SCAMS: SWEEPSTAKES OR LOTTERY SCAMS

Notifications sent in the mail or via email with a name that looks and sounds like a government agency or some other official looking authority telling you that you've just won a significant amount of money should be looked at with suspicion. Indeed, many times these notifications come with a check. To claim your winnings in this sweepstakes, you must deposit the check and pay upfront taxes and processing fees. You may even be asked for your bank routing and account information so a money transfer can occur. However, once you have complied with the request, the result is the theft of your money and your identity!

HOW TO PROTECT YOURSELF AGAINST SWEEPSTAKE SCAMS

Scammers often target the elderly because of the perception that older people are vulnerable, too trusting, or unaware of the scams. So you and everyone is at risk!

REMEMBER: If you did not play the lottery or enter a sweepstakes or contest, you didn't win one. And, legitimate sweepstakes will never ask for money up front from winners!

TELEMARKETING SCAMS

What to do if your phone rings and the person says:

"You've won one of five valuable prizes"

"If you buy our product, you'll get a free bonus"

"You've been specially selected (for this offer)"

"We'll just put your shipping and handling charges on your credit card"

"This offer goes away if you don't make up your mind right away"

Say **"No, thank you,"** and hang up. Afterward, you should contact the Office of Attorney General in your state and file a formal complaint.

Telemarketing scammers bait their customers using fake prizes, products or services such as free or low cost vacation trip packages. They also use payday loan and credit card protection schemes, recent disaster relief campaigns, out of country lotteries, and extended car warranties which can be especially attractive to consumers during times when the economy is down.

HOW TO PROTECT YOURSELF AGAINST TELEMARKETER SCAMS

Begin by asking yourself who is calling you and what do they want. Telemarketers have to tell you it is a sales call and give you the option of opting out BEFORE they make their sales presentation. If you don't hear them say it is a sales call, say **"No Thanks"** and hang up.

Telemarketers can be very fast talkers which is a red flag to you that they may be hiding something. Slow them down and take your time because legitimate businesses will give you extra time and written information if they want you to commit to buying their product or service. And, ask yourself: if what they are offering is free, why are they asking you to pay? Ask them that question because free is free. If they want payment, the product or service is no longer a free prize or a free gift.

If the telemarketer already has your account information in front of them, they will not need to confirm your account. Beware that they may be attempting to get you to say yes to approving a change you do not want to make to your account.

If you don't want a business to call you again, tell the telemarketer not to call again and then register your landline and mobile phone numbers with your state Do Not Call Registry and with the National Do Not Call Registry at 1-888-382-1222. Once your phone numbers have been registered with the Federal Trade Commission, most telemarketers should not call once your numbers have been on the registry for 31 days. If they call, you can file a complaint at www.donotcall.gov.

GRANDPARENT SCAMS

This type of scam is the most devious because it touches the Senior's heart through their most treasured asset – their grandchildren. The telephone rings and a telephone scammer, who may have secured your grandchild's names from social media or internet sites, says, "Grand mom, it's me . . . please don't tell my parents." This exchange reveals the actual name of your grandchild. The voice, which could also he disguised as a lawyer or police officer goes on to say the family member is out of time and needs money right away for bail, to pay for emergency car repairs, an emergency hospital bill or to pay the fare for a ticket to come home. Because the caller has asked you not to tell their parents and you're the only person he can ask to wire him the money, you may not question whether the emergency actually exists. Be aware! If you're not certain the call is legitimate, don't follow through on what is being requested. By all means, call the parent you've been asked not to call.

CHARITY SCAMS

A scammer calls you on your phone or knocks on your door and asks for donations to a well-known charity. You are proud to say you know this charity. What you don't know is he has tricked and confused you by taking advantage of a charity with a good reputation by making a slight change to the name or logo of a charity which sounds so familiar to you so you don't notice that it's not the charity you think it is.

HOW TO PROTECT YOURSELF AGAINST CHARITY SCAMS:

Before responding to a charity's request for help do these things: 1) Ask for a printed copy or a website link to the charity's annual report. The reason you want that is to find out what the charity does with the donations it receives and how much of your donation goes to help the people and programs they say they serve; 2) Make sure you agree with the values of the charity and ask yourself if you agree with the goals of the charity; 3) Do not allow yourself to be pressured into giving. Sad stories and high pressure tactics can be signal that the charity could be corrupt or dishonest, 4) If you do decide to give in person, never give using a credit card or cash on the spot. Write a check made payable to the charity, not the individual asking for your donation, and send the check directly to the charity's address.

INSURANCE SCAMS

Insurance scams may not be as obvious as other scams for the simple reason that we, the consumers, play a significant role in how these types of scams affect our spending. We know and understand the necessity of purchasing homeowners', automobile or renters' insurances, but too many times, motivated by fear, we are prone to buy too much insurance or coverages that are unnecessary, duplicates of other coverage or wasteful.

Single-purpose coverages such as accidental death, cancer and credit card fraud policies are not good deals especially when they are compared with the amount you could pay for them ($1.00 per thousand) and the amount you receive back (10-15 cents per thousand) when a claim is filed. [Note: Seniors: You may want to exercise this same rationale when it comes to calculating the ratios between how much you spend playing lotteries compared to how much you win. You do not want to bust your budget!].

Deductibles can also be a mystery to unwary consumers if you don't understand that you can be biased during the sales pitch – one that highlights the accident, illness or theft -- and react accordingly by choosing the wrong deductibles. Instead of making rational decisions based on the actual damage amounts you could incur, you might purchase insurances based on possible losses, worries, and fears. A good rule of thumb would be to choose a high deductible over a small deductible.

Recently, after giving serious thought to our age, retirement income and the remaining balance on our home mortgage, we decided to sell our home and move into an apartment. Our move, ended up taking place before the sale of our home because the first sale fizzled out just days before closing. That meant we had to arrange for renters' insurance while at the same time paying for mortgage insurance. The house eventually sold, and three months later we only had one residence for which we were financially responsible. A few weeks later, when comparing our budgeted insurance costs, we realized we were paying double for our renters' insurance. That was remedied when we dropped the amount of coverage from $150,000 to $50,000 based on the fact that we no longer needed coverage for $150,000 worth of household furnishings.

The following list includes several insurance policies you can probably live without or reduce the amount of your coverage. Of course, the choice is always yours Seniors:

1) **Accidental death insurance** (buy enough life insurance so it covers all circumstances)

2) **Automobile collision** (this is wasteful if your vehicle is an older vehicle or if you have a DUI, DWI, tickets or accidents on your driving record)

3) **Automobile medical** (no need to buy more since this is most likely already on your auto insurance policy and health insurance pays first anyway)

4) **Credit card insurance** (your money is better spent staying out of credit card debt)

5) **Credit card fraud insurance** (there are federal, bank and credit card issuer safeguards in place. You should read your statements carefully and call the credit card company if your card is lost, stolen or something else is wrong)

6) **Extended warranties** (these are not a good deal since manufacturers' warranties covers your item so don't allow sales pitches or your worries to rule here)

7) **Flight insurance** (if you must have coverage, buy a cheap term life policy instead)

8) **Flood insurance** (hardly anything is covered except your furnace and appliances or if you live in a floodplain or have a walk-out basement)

9) **Rental car damage insurance** (if you have full coverage on at least one vehicle, your auto coverage extends automatically to a rented car. If no full auto coverage, your home-life-auto insurance may cover this and your credit card company may cover if rental is charged to that credit card.)

IDENTITY THEFT

Identity theft consists of fraudulent purchases and use of a person's private identifying information, usually for financial gain. This happens when someone lures you under false pretenses to reveal your personal data such as your social security number, birth certificate, PIN or credit card and other financial account numbers to access your credit and bank accounts, medical care or other aspects of your finances. This information can also be obtained when someone rummages through your trash and your mailbox or steals your pre-approved credit card solicitations to apply for credit in your name without you knowing that it has happened.

HOW TO PROTECT YOURSELF AGAINST IDENTITY THEFT

Following is a 10-point checklist for protecting yourself against identity theft. Please pay close attention to these steps. They could help you to avoid becoming the next victim.

1. Remember that banks, credit card companies, and government offices never call you to verify your personal or account information. Likewise, law enforcement agencies will not contact you to demand payment of fines over the phone or internet.

2. Keep documentation such as your social security card, birth certificate, passport and other identification documents in a secure place and avoid keeping digital copies unsecured on cloud storage. Note: It would be a splendid idea to designate A "Legacy" file or drawer located where your family members know where to access your information in the event of your death.

3. Make sure to review monthly financial statements and bills. Make it a priority to shred sensitive documents as soon as you can to include receipts, bills and subscription labels. Shredding on a regular basis will help protect you from someone

accessing your garbage and will help you not to hoard or allow your documents pile up.

4. Make contact with appropriate businesses to ask about any unexpected bills or charges you may have received.

5. Have photocopies made of your licenses, bank and credit cards, etc., and put them in a secure place (Legacy file or drawer).

6. Be alert when using your debit and credit cards in stores and restaurants. When you arrive home or before going out, empty your purse and wallet of extra credit cards and your social security card. If you discover your debit or credit card is missing, immediately make a report that it is lost or stolen.

7. Personal Identification Numbers called PINs should be memorized and should never be written on your cards or on anything in your purse or wallet. Consider using phrases with numbers when choosing a new PIN.

8. Call 1-888-5-OPT-OUT (1-888-567-8688) to stop credit card companies from sending you pre-approved applications to your home.

9. If you learn that you are a victim of identity theft, immediately file a report with your local police, immediately alert your banks and credit card

accounts and immediately contact the credit reporting bureaus so that a fraud alert can be issued.

10. Request your free annual credit report, which can be obtained online by searching for free annual credit report or by phone at 1-877-322-8228 at least once a year from providers (Equifax, Experian, and TransUnion). If you get one report every four months from each reporting agency you will end up with a full year of credit reports for free!

CHAPTER 3

SHALT THOU OWN A HOME?

There was a couple I knew, now deceased, who when I first met them lived in a large ranch house in a suburban neighborhood. It was a beautiful house built on land they had purchased in their young adult years when they were owners of a prospering small business. The land had been purchased from a close relative who owned a construction company. The house was located on a corner lot at the intersection of two streets, one of which was actually named for the husband and both the land and the home represented a proud legacy for this family. I can still remember their spacious home and the large yard where I joined them for some of their family gatherings.

Many years later, after reaching their senior years, it became evident that downsizing was inevitable. Making this difficult decision had become necessary because the husband was experiencing declining health from many years of alcoholism and from years of making poor financial choices in their business ventures. They also did not have retirement savings or investments to fall back on. This large home was in disrepair and the couple's income was not enough to sustain it. So, without any other alternative options, the couple turned their home over to their youngest son.

Within several years the son's irresponsibility and a lack of interest in owning or maintaining the home, it went up for sale for back taxes. Their final years were lived comfortably in an apartment in an area close to family members, stores and medical facilities and where the wife's small retirement income and their combined social security benefits gave them some financial peace even though there was some regret about the home they lost.

THE GOLDEN YEARS

The couple in our story began with a mental picture in their hearts of their "golden years". During the many years the husband worked in the construction trades, becoming a business owner and the years the wife worked for a local school district, they probably had ideas of how their retirement would play out. How those years would include enjoying themselves while living comfortably without financial worries in their own home. Nowhere in this scenario could they envision a struggle of any kind brought on by inflation, failure to make sound savings or investment decisions, and chronic illness. Instead, like so many seniors today, they found themselves in survival mode facing the sudden reality that owning a home was no longer a viable option.

Realistically, the answer to the question of whether you should rent or own is one that cannot be answered by anyone but you. My recommendation would be for you and your family to know the facts, the benefits, and the pros and cons of owning or renting – to make a plan, and to budget your income to accommodate that plan sooner rather than later.

Today, there are many seniors living month to month on social security benefits averaging $1,262 per month, and many seniors receiving less than that. According to the U.S. Census Bureau, the median income for the elderly age 65-74 is $36,320; for those 74 and older that drops to $25,417, and 12% of seniors 65 and older are at poverty level).

Millions of households today spend more than half their monthly income on rent and mortgage payments, one of which includes mortgage insurance and property taxes while the other includes renters' insurance. This presents a serious dilemma when spending too much on housing drives you to take on debt you cannot afford.

Like the couple in our story and the many other seniors who live on limited incomes and resources, housing is your single highest month to month expense. Considering that fact, it isn't difficult to see how someone could lose their home, especially when they keep falling behind in their payments because of allowing their housing costs to take up too much of their income. For instance, let's say housing is approximately 35% of your monthly income. Personal insurance and pensions are another 5% and health care 14%. Transportation (est. 14.2%); food (est. 12.4%), and miscellaneous/other (est. 19.7%) round out expenses, which leaves microscopic room for excess. It paints a pretty grim future where many are using high-interest credit cards for groceries and medical bills.

Thankfully, money management is one of life's biggest challenges that we can control, and since money is one of the main topics on people's minds, we can look to budgeting as one of our greatest weapons against those challenges.

If your budget requires a short-term boost and you are willing and physically able to sacrifice something to remain in your home, you can consider working on the side, on weekends, or give up some luxuries like eating out, some more expensive social activities (casinos and lotteries) or vacations for whatever time it takes for you to get back on track.

TO OWN OR RENT

When young adults buy a home, it is a vessel for building memories with family and friends. A house roots you in a community. Home ownership has the extra benefit of building equity that can be transferred generationally. On the downside, homeowners could lose the advantages of retirement savings, goals for travel and other social activities if they don't ensure that their expenses are kept low.

Seniors who decide to downsize may find that switching costs between a mortgage payment versus that of rent is not only a cheaper and more flexible alternative but, after some wise research, they may find that moving to another location altogether is best for the lifestyle they choose to live.

Another consideration for the renting vs buying debate is the fact that currently 77% of the housing demand is being generated by the 10,000 baby boomers turning 65 every day. As of the year 2030, the biggest challenge facing these baby boomers will be finding affordable housing.

In this section of *Essential Practical Wisdom for Seniors*, we wanted to specifically address those baby boomers who do not have paid off homes and who will not have the kind of long-term economic options enjoyed by many of their parents. Our goal is also to assist the members of this group, specifically those who find it difficult to make ends meet, to be emotionally ready to make necessary decisions for the lifestyle changes necessary to enjoy their golden years.

I believe that the fundamental ingredient to enjoying your personal golden years is to learn to live on a modest income.

INTRODUCTION TO HOME REPAIRS

A few months prior to completing this section of the Senior's Guide to Spending, my mother who turns 90 this year decided she wanted some work done on her home. Her decision, based on a wish list she's had for some time, came alive when she was visited by a contractor who went door to door in her neighborhood. The contractor also mentioned that he has done work on behalf of a local department store in her area which was a name she recognized having purchased many items from them over many years. To insure that this was not a home repair scam, my Mom and my sister, who happened to be with her that day, listened to the contractor's pitch and phoned me to get my email address so he could send me a list of the work he was willing to do, the timeframe for that work and the estimates. I also requested that he email me a list of references as well as the insurance documentation we would need. Within a few days, we had everything we needed for my Mom to give her approval for the work she wanted done.

Eventually, the first projects requested were done to my Mom's complete joy and satisfaction. We are grateful that this was not a home repair scam, and my Mom was pleased with the work that was done and how the contractor kept his word to do the job professionally and promptly. Unfortunately, this is not always the case. While many home repair contractors operate legitimate businesses, many deceive and defraud people out of large sums of money.

HOME REPAIR SCAMS

There are many Seniors who report Home Repair Scams to their local authorities. In those unfortunate cases, someone knocks at the door or calls on the phone offering to make repairs, some of which are in need of immediate attention and should not be ignored. What was the difference between my Mother's home repair experience and that of someone whose been scammed?

1.) The Senior client should refrain from using a contractor who has no experience performing the type of home repair needed. He should have a relative or a friend who can ask the right questions, request the information and/or set a timeframe for decision making. This is crucial when dealing with a fast talking scammer who can apply pressure by using confusing language and fear tactics by saying the repairs must be handled immediately.

2.) A scammer may not be an established local business, duly licensed or insured. His proposal may sound too good to be true and he may not offer a written estimate or contract. He may build the Senior's confidence by saying he is doing work in the Senior's neighborhood and has extra materials left from other projects he could use to cut the cost. If not specifically asked, the scammer does not offer references and, even if he does, his references may not be reachable.

3.) A scammer should be avoided if he asks you to secure the required building permits for the work he's to do or demands that you pay him in cash or pay him in full before work is done on your home.

4.) A red flag should go up if the contractor asks the Senior for money for materials *before* he starts the work. Remember: A reputable, reliable contractor should be able to buy his materials on credit and should be able to provide you a schedule to include an initial down payment and a list of your incremental payments until the work is completed.

5.) Avoid anyone who tells you there's no need for a written contract. By law, all contracts for $500 of more must be in writing. In fact, it's a great idea to request a written contract no matter what the contract amount.

6.) Withhold final payment until you have completed a thorough walk through, are satisfied that all the work you've requested has been done and have received any documents such as a certificate of occupancy or inspection reports, if applicable.

HOW TO PROTECT YOURSELF AGAINST HOME REPAIR SCAMS

In addition to the actions suggested in the above paragraphs, you have the right to cancel a home repair contract within three (3) business days except for emergency repairs or services. In addition, you can contact your local Better Business Bureau, the Chamber of Commerce or the Bureau of Consumer Protection if you feel a need to check further on the contractor before signing a contract for his services.

HOME INSURANCE PLANS AND HOW TO SAVE MONEY FOR NECESSARY COVERAGES

Recently we decided to revisit our insurance coverages since we sold our home. We found out our auto insurance was excellent, but our renter's insurance was too expensive. It seems our agent wrote a policy with enough coverage to cover the price of our home, appliances, and furnishings. Now that we are renters, we were able to significantly reduce our insurance costs since we own fewer things. If you follow the principles of Essential Practical Wisdom and embrace a lifestyle of minimalism, you will save too. Review your coverage at renewal time or if you make a significant change in your living arrangements to make sure your insurance needs haven't changed.

CHAPTER 4

SAVING ON GROCERY AND HOLIDAY SHOPPING

As a senior citizen, it is not only important to use your household income wisely but just as important to take advantage of all the discount privileges available to you as well.

Considering our current economic condition, spending less money will mean more savings to you. It is reported that senior citizens spend on an average of 12.4% of their median annual income on food. With the increase of the prevalence of obesity for both men and women over the past fifteen years between 1999-2002 and 2011-2014, many seniors living on fixed incomes are spending more of their time and attention on shopping in healthier and more cost effective ways.

Many stores offer senior citizen discounts but do not advertise them. Some stores don't even give you the discount automatically unless you ask for it. So, be sure to ask! Even if you're required to travel a longer distance and have to make a greater effort, finding the best prices will reap great dividends for your pocketbook and health. Today, the variety of stores to shop in can include ethnic markets, dollar stores, retail supercenters and farmers' markets.

Here are several important ways you can experience money savings that can potentially save you thousands of dollars annually:

- **Make a list and stick to it.** Be sure to write down the items you need before going shopping. Not knowing what you want ahead of time can make you spend more. When you are prepared with a list, you can eliminate most unnecessary purchases.

- **Compare the prices of your local stores with other stores in your area**. You may be surprised to find you can save by shopping for your preferred items in the cheaper stores.

- **Do not shop for groceries when you're hungry.** If you're hungry, you will end up buying more than you actually need.

- **Sign up for free rewards programs.** Even if you're not a frequent shopper in the store offering rewards, you may be able to save on reduced items marked down specifically for reward card holders.

- **If shopping online, search the web for online coupon codes and discounts.** There are many discount sites that have coupons or codes for your favorite products, so take advantage of the savings!

- **Buy frozen fruits and vegetables and "in season" produce.** These items will keep for a long time, will minimize waste, and can guarantee you have a supply of healthier foods on hand whenever the need arises. If you need fresh produce, always purchase in season selections. Buying in season produce can save you money and you can actually see that the colorful produce you're buying is fresh and firm.

HOLIDAY SHOPPING TIPS

No matter what time of the year, it's always wise to plan your shopping trips wisely. While you may have once enjoyed the rush of a wild day of shopping, it becomes a lot less fun as a senior and can present unwanted challenges for older shoppers. So, plan your shopping trips well, especially during the holiday season. Stay away from shopping the days just before a holiday and just after a holiday. Instead, shop on calmer days during non-peak times like early morning or late afternoon.

Going shopping with others can be a smart thing to do and can help you with shopping ideas for loved ones. It can also be a cost-savings on transportation costs.

Senior citizens can also consider shopping online in the comfort and convenience of your own home or can take advantage of a tech-savvy grandson or other family member to do it for you online where you can access special offers, discounts and free shipping.

SECTION II

ESSENTIAL PRACTICAL SPENDING IN HEALTH & WELLNESS

CHAPTER 5

HEALTHCARE DOS & DON'TS

When it comes to living an optimal life as you age, one place where you cannot afford to cut corners is your health. Let's face it: we are living longer lives and it is important to live healthier lives as well. That means focusing on physical and emotional health as we age- committing to exercise, meditation, and of course making sure that you have superior healthcare. Spending wisely can ensure that you are never faced with unexpected emergencies that impede your quality of life. Embracing Essential Practical Wisdom means that you also embrace the best version of you.

Let's review some common and not so common ways to save money on health and wellness:

HEALTHCARE SAVINGS DOLLARS AND COMMON SENSE

According to the Administration on Aging by 2060 there will be 98 million older people, more than double what there are currently (source: aoa.gov). That staggering number highlights why obtaining affordable healthcare will remain a challenge for aging people for decades to come. Today, most older Americans spend an average of nearly $6,000 annually in out of pocket expenses for healthcare, which is a very large amount. Finding ways to save and spend wisely, as previous chapters showed, is key, but we also suggest adopting saving strategies that specifically focus on healthcare related expenses.

HEALTHCARE DO #1 - RESEARCH AND NEGOTIATE PRICING ON ALL HEALTHCARE RELATED EXPENSES.

Here is a familiar scenario for many older people: You have just retired from your job that offered premium healthcare resources with minimal deductibles and an option to put aside portions of your salary on a pre-tax basis for health-related expenses. What you soon find out is that none of those cushy benefits transfer over with you into retirement. There is no pre-tax fund, your out of pocket expenses have tripled and you find that routine preventative care, such as a trip to the dentist, is costing thousands of dollars and you have no way of paying for it. So, what do you do? Well, for many older people the choice is to forego regular full healthcare or forego healthcare all together which can worsen preexisting conditions and lead to premature death. There is no reason for this to happen to you. If you are willing and able to go to your local library and research different health related options in your community, you can avoid lapses in health coverage.

HEALTHCARE DON'T – NOT SAVING FOR A RAINY DAY

Now more than ever before, you must make sure that you have money put aside for health and wellness. The more you save the more you don't have to be caught off guard when an unexpected health related expense occurs. Take my friend Karen for example. Karen was a vibrant, active senior married to an equally active husband. Both were in excellent health and put most of their extra income towards vacations and new clothes. Then one day, the unthinkable happened: Karen and her husband were on their way back home from an evening bible study when a car swerved into their lane and caused a head on collision. Both Karen and her husband faced devastating injuries that caused them to be bedridden for months. Unfortunately, because they didn't have any money saved for healthcare, they ended up with mounting debt that forced them to sell their house and move in with their daughter in another state. Suddenly their luxurious life was gone.

The moral of this story is that you truly never know what will happen in your life, so it is best to be wise with your money and put some away each month. One way to save is to open a Medical Savings Account (MSA). If you are on Medicare, you can do an MSA Plan coupled with a high deductible health plan. Alternatively, you can open a regular savings account and have a portion of your income automatically deposited into the account. Whatever you do, find ways to make regular savings towards healthcare expenses.

The most important thing to remember is this: When it comes to healthcare, you need to be empowered.

HEALTHCARE DO: USE FREE RESOURCES AVAILABLE TO SENIORS FOR HEALTHCARE

Did you know in the state of Pennsylvania and in the state of Washington there are Senior Farmers Market nutrition programs that provides healthy meals to low-income adults over the age of 60? Did you also know that in New York City there is a program called Big Apple Rx that offers prescription savings at more than 2,000 pharmacies? The truth is that in cities and towns big and small, there are great programs that provide discounts to seniors for healthcare related expenses. A good way to find these discounts is to contact your local Department of Aging offices or visit their website and look in the "Resources" section for free or low-cost services.

The number one place to find resources for seniors is your local senior center. The days of the senior center being boring places to play bingo are long gone. Today's senior centers provide state of the art resources, many of which are at no cost to you. Healthcare providers will often provide services specifically to senior centers such as flu shots and counseling services

HEALTHCARE DON'T: FAILING TO ORGANIZE AND KEEP TRACK OF MEDICAL EXPENSES AND HEALTH HISTORY

As you age, the importance of keeping good records becomes crystal clear. There will be days where you forget critical things that you use to remember with ease, things like the number of prescriptions you have or your doctor's first name. You may have a hard time keeping track of what bills you have paid and what bills are still outstanding. The life of the senior revolves around using optimal organizational skills to make up for the things we lose as we age. Whether you use a detailed spreadsheet or simple pencil and paper, organizing medical information and expenses pays off in the long-term. It can also be a help to you or to a relative who accompanies you to your doctor appointments or provides other record keeping assistance as you age.

Case Study: Rebecca Reynolds is a 75-year old widowed mother of three and grandmother of eight! When her husband Frank died three years ago after a lengthy illness, Rebecca was faced with overwhelming debt and her husband's disorganization through the years in keeping track of expenses. In their younger years, Frank had been a reliable steward of the couple's finances, but as his illness progressed, he wasn't able to keep track of bills and payments. Rebecca, who had never taken a proactive approach in paying attention to financial matters, only learned of the magnitude of the debt she faced a few months after Frank's death. Rebecca was despondent and unsure of what she could do until she found a free financial literacy counseling class at her local senior center. Over the course of a few sessions, Rebecca learned that there were services available to her to aid her as she transitioned to her new life as a single woman.

Over the course of six months Rebecca sought out the services of a professional organizer who helped her sort through her husband's records. She started using a simple printable template that organized bills as paid or unpaid. She worked with bill collectors to negotiate on past due bills and was able to use a portion of her savings to pay all outstanding bills and debt. As Rebecca became more financially literate and organized, she found that her overall decision-making skills were improved in her own healthcare matters. Rebecca, for instance, signed up for a service with her primary care provider to have online access to her health and payment history to back up for her physical files. She carried on a filing system of sorting paid, in progress, and overdue bills, making sure to avoid the latter. Finally, she started working at her senior center to help others with the knowledge she had gained on organizing medical information as an adviser. "I cannot stress enough the importance of keeping organized records" Rebecca said, "It has changed my life."

CHAPTER 6

INVESTING IN AN ACTIVE LIFE

Like clockwork Ernestine Shepherd wakes up usually between the hours of 3:00- 4:00 AM and runs 10 miles. She is also a professional bodybuilder with 10% body fat and six-pack abs. Her diet consists of lean meats and plenty of fruits and vegetables What makes her healthy lifestyle even more admirable is that Ernestine is in her eighties and in better shape than people half her age!

Older Americans like Ernestine illustrate that age is truly just a number, and that it is never too late to invest in wellness. A commitment to a healthy lifestyle that involves exercise is a critical component of a lifestyle that embraces *Essential Practical Wisdom* because it can help you avoid or delay the preventable diseases and ailments that many older people face such as diabetes, high blood pressure, arthritis, and cardiovascular disease.

You don't have to become a world-class bodybuilder to live an optimal life, but what you can do is make incremental changes day by day that will help you live a longer and healthier life. This is an investment that pays in dividends!

According to the World Health Organization, it is recommended that older people aim for 150 minutes of moderate-intensity aerobic activity. A good measurement for determining if an activity is moderate-intensity would be to check if you are able to hold a conversation with frequent breaths. In addition, your heart rate should be elevated, and you break a sweat.

If you are not able to hold a conversation or are completely out of breath, you are most likely working out at too high an intensity. If you don't feel challenged at all and your breath is at its normal frequency, then you should work a little bit harder. It is all about balance.

A healthier lifestyle does not need to break the bank. As you will see, you already have access to plenty of resources that promote wellness for free or low-costs. As mentioned, many times in this book, if you research what is available in your local community you will find that there are organizations that want to help you with nutrition care, food resources, and exercise programming. As always, please consult your medical provider before beginning any type of physical activity program. You may have an underlying condition that prevents you from doing intense exercise so you should get a thorough check-out from your doctor to make sure you can handle exercise.

SILVERSNEAKERS® FITNESS PROGRAMS

Specifically targeting senior citizens, SilverSneakers® is an innovative health and fitness program that most major Medicare carriers participate in. Membership in SilverSneakers® provides you with access to thousands of fitness facilities across the United States. You also get access to a variety of fitness classes, walking programs, and aerobic classes.

Along with access to fitness programs and facilities, SilverSneakers® has an app that you can install on your smartphone where you can access fitness exercises and track your activity.

Not sure if a fitness center participates in SilverSneakers®? All you have to do is call or ask someone at the facility you are interested in joining. You have nothing to lose and everything to gain by taking advantage of this program.

HOW ONE MARRIED COUPLE FOUND THEIR FOUNTAIN OF YOUTH AT THE LOCAL REC CENTER

Carl and Marjorie have been married for 35 years and are recent retirees who just had their youngest child start college. What they found with their empty nest was that a sedentary lifestyle quickly took over. Marjorie would spend her days watching her ever-growing collection of DVDs while Carl would spend all day playing solitaire on his computer. Pretty soon, both found that even the most routine of physical activities, such as walking up a flight of stairs or walking through the grocery store, left them tired and winded. They also both got alarming diagnoses from their doctor: Marjorie found out she had heart failure and Carl type 2 diabetes. They knew a change was needed, but felt that they couldn't afford gym memberships on a limited budget. Through a conversation with another couple at their church, they discovered that a rec center that the church worked with and participated in the SilverSneakers® program and that they had access to a modern gym with an Olympic sized pool and nutrition classes.

Over time Carl and Marjorie worked up to doing some form of physical activity for 30 minutes four days a week and the results were incredible. Carl was able to come off of the insulin he had been prescribed for his type 2 diabetes and Marjorie was able slow the progression of her heart failure, adding years to her life.

With their newfound commitment to fitness, Carl and Marjorie have seen their outlook on life improve as well. "We are happier than we ever have been" Carl said, "We wake up every morning excited for the day ahead."

CHAPTER 7

PHYSICAL ACTIVITY IN THE HOME AND NEIGHBORHOOD

For many, the idea of working out at a gym may be uncomfortable and more challenging, but as you age, physical activity becomes a must to maintain your levels of energy and vitality. For many, that may mean forgoing a gym membership all together and creating a fitness program for home. If this is you, I have some great tips for getting physically active in the home and in your neighborhood so there are no excuses to be a couch potato!

WALKING WITH FRIENDS IN YOUR NEIGHBORHOOD

Sally Johns, 68, is a recent retiree who wanted to stay active in her new lifestyle, but always hated gyms. "Ever since grade school" Sally said, "the thought of going to a gym made me apprehensive so I always found ways to be physically fit outdoors." For Sally this meant hiking, playing tennis, golf, and of course walking. As her income diminished, she looked for ways to save on activities and found out that there was already a great walking program in her neighborhood. Now every day at 6:00 AM Sally and her friends Kelly and Martina put on their walking shoes and walk for one hour in the morning and another 30 minutes at night after dinner.

Don't have a walking program in your neighborhood? Why not start one! It is a great way to create community with your neighbors, stay fit, and improve your quality of life. Another tip: if you are walking early mornings or in the evening, always walk with a partner and make sure you walk in well-lit and safe areas.

OTHER WAYS TO WORK OUT IN THE HOME

Doing exercises at home can be great for changing our moods especially during rainy days and in the winter months when it's not feasible to be outdoors. You can do physical activity in the home alone or with a workout partner. Some examples of stimulating exercises that can be done in the home are as follows:

- Mild aerobic exercises and jogging in place can be great for increasing your endurance, heart rate and promoting proper breathing.

- Light weightlifting using light weights or canned food strengthens muscles and becomes even more beneficial as you age.

- Balancing exercises help to prevent falls by centering you physically and improving your overall balance.

- Stretching when you get up in the morning, at night before bed helps to prevent injuries and keeps your body more flexible.

- Chair yoga offers a myriad of positions to provide you with a full-body exercise routine all while sitting down. It is also a great way to incorporate meditation with the lights dimmed and quiet music playing. Be careful though, you might fall asleep!

SECTION III

ESSENTIAL PRACTICAL WISDOM IN PURCHASING PRODUCTS AND SERVICES

CHAPTER 8

SAVING DOLLARS ON CELL PHONES

Anyone who has had cell phone service any length of time has experienced the shock of expecting a cheap phone bill only to be surprised by fees and other charges that drive up the costs for this service.

Recently I was in a local phone store of a major carrier. There was a senior citizen there with her daughter. The conversation I overheard between her and the store clerk broke my heart.

"You have to speak to me in a way I understand. I only went to the second grade. I don't have a Ph.D. like some of you people," the older woman said.

I could tell by the worried tone of her voice that she was somewhat flustered, even with her grown daughter standing at her side. The older woman was clearly upset and embarrassed with her phone bill being too high and she wanted to make sure it didn't happen again.

Just like this senior citizen, if at all possible, I recommend going to the store in person when making a cell phone purchase. Make sure you allow enough minutes to get fully caught up. You do not want to pay a high initial bill. Just think about all those family and friends who will be delighted you have a new cell phone. Remember to ask if you can lower your monthly allowances later.

Please be aware that it is your responsibility to make sure that your cell phone bill does not exceed the amount you desire. This is what the woman in the story above encountered and, for her, it was a budget buster. Overage charges and fees on your cell phone bill are tough to swallow, especially when they are unexpected and result from patterns of use you thought were safe and well within your plan. If you are familiar with data and text plans enough to know your usage patterns, talk with your cell phone provider to figure out what the best plan for your needs will be.

CELL PHONE OPTIONS FOR SENIORS

If you don't text and aren't interested in accessing the internet away from home, you don't need a data plan.

A voice only plan may be enough for you. If this is the case, you will not need a smartphone. A smartphone is a cell phone that functions as a mini computer with a touchscreen, internet access, and apps.

Before selecting a mobile phone, it is helpful to understand how you will use your phone for voice calls. Are you only going to use your phones to make calls? Then you don't need the latest smartphone with the latest tech features. Do you frequently text with friends and family? Maybe a phone with a larger screen is a good idea so you can type with a larger keyboard. Try to make a list of three options you definitely want for your phone before you buy it.

If you find that over time you consistently get overage charges, I recommend contacting your cell phone provider and getting a higher data plan. Don't be afraid to negotiate to lower the price or to get other features you want bundled in for free. Cell phone companies are in the business of pleasing customers so they will work with you if you have reasonable requests.

All of the major cell phone providers offer exclusive phones and plans geared towards seniors. But, beware of "upsells" (sales techniques to convince you to purchase more expensive items, upgrades or other items) when you shop. As a rule, get the basic plan and phone. If you plan on texting, you should get a smartphone. Most seniors only need the phones designated for seniors. You can get a good smartphone for less than $100. Watch for specials and last year models which can save you up to 50% or more off the price of the current model.

WHY THE "FREE TABLET" ISN'T ALWAYS FREE

Many phone companies are now bundling tablets such as iPad and Galaxy tablets in their plans. Beware of these because they use data when purchased from phone companies. If you buy a tablet, I recommend one that is Wi-Fi only. This will remove the temptation to overuse your data plan watching movies and spying on the grandkids on social media while out running errands and unexpectedly using up your data. Remember; most public places such as doctor's offices and grocery stores have free Wi-Fi. Even fast-food places have free wi-fi and many open air spaces like parks do as well. Always look for ways to save the data for the times when you absolutely need it!

One more thing I recommend when it comes to cell phones is limiting social media use on the phone. I love keeping up with my grandkids and friends from school too, but remember that Facebook and Twitter use data on your phone. I recommend not installing social media apps on your phone for this reason. Log on to these sites on your secured home internet when you have free time. All those notifications, messages, and "pokes" use up tons of data, not to mention your valuable time. And be sure to let your grands know your phone has boundaries.

CHAPTER 9

PURCHASING A CAR

Personally, I am of the opinion that seniors should NOT buy a new car. Remember, cars lose most of their value in the first few years. Buying a new car is proof that you are not utilizing *Essential Practical Wisdom*. Remember: you don't have to keep up with the Jones' anymore. You have nothing to prove. Buy a car that is dependable and that gets you where you need to go. I recommend that it be at least 2 years old. If, in the future, I write a book titled *Essential Practical Wisdom for Seniors: Car-Buying* I will delve more in depth into how you should approach car buying and maintenance in your golden years. But, until then, here are some brief tips:

BUYING A USED CAR

There is a lot of research involved in using practical wisdom when car shopping. You can do most of this research online and if you lack access to your own computer you can do this through libraries and bookstores. If you empower yourself with knowledge, you will make better decisions. Remember there are various types of used car deals so do some homework before you start shopping for a used car. It may save you serious money later.

If the research process seems overwhelming, you may want to consider hiring one of your adult grandchildren or another dependable young person to help you with your search. Make sure they are familiar with computers and can save you time researching. Give them your list of features you want based on your initial research and tell them to give you 3-4 car options. Again, tell them you do NOT want a brand-new car.

Ask yourself several questions before you begin your car search. For example, what amount have you budgeted for your used car purchase? Consider your driving habits. What will the car be used for? Do you really need your own car? Sites like DMV.org and Carfax provide great car buying checklists that are helpful for knowing what to look for and you should consult resources like this before going to a dealership.

Used car selling rules in the US require sellers to post buyer's guides on every used car they offer for sale. A buyer's guide will let you know if the car has any issues that aren't readily apparent by just looking at it. Get all promises in writing and keep the buyer's guide for reference after the sale.

We recommend that you ask to have the car inspected by an independent mechanic before you buy. You should get an inspection on a car, even if it is listed as "certified" to make sure you haven't been ripped off. This should cost about $100, and it is money well spent.

If you buy a car from a private individual or at an auction, I also recommend getting as much verifiable background information on the car as possible. There are unscrupulous people out there who sell "lemons" or junk cars to unsuspecting older people every day. Don't be a victim. If a deal seems too good to be true, it is! If someone is not willing to share information with you about a car, that is a warning sign that something isn't right.

WISE CAR PAYMENT OPTIONS

When purchasing your car, you will have one of two payment choices – to pay in full or to finance over time.

Financing your purchase will increase the amount you pay over time. You must also consider how much of a down payment you can make, the monthly payment, the financing terms (e.g., 36 months, 48 months or more), and the annual percentage rate (APR). Rates will be higher if you decide to finance your purchase for a shorter period on used cars rather than a new one. Before signing an auto financing agreement, make sure you understand all of the terms and that the monthly payment and insurance combined never exceeds 10% of your monthly income.

CAR INSURANCE

What you pay in car insurance is usually determined in part by factors such as the likelihood of vandalism or theft, the cost to repair it and the total value of the car. Most insurers have discounts for alarms and anti-theft locks, even automatic seatbelts. A good driving record can also save you money. Here are some tips for saving money on car insurance:

1) Negotiate with the insurance providers by getting multiple quotes and picking the provider with the best deal.

2) Ask for a higher deductible to make your monthly payment lower. If you budget, the higher deductible will not be an issue.

3) An excellent way to find a deal on car

insurance is to ask friends and family.

4) Bundle insurance. Your auto, home, flood
    insurance can all be on one bill, and most
    insurers will give you a nice discount for
    doing this.

CHAPTER 10

TELEVISION AND CABLE
SERVICES AND ALTERNATIVES

Before downsizing and selling our home, my husband and I were paying almost $200 a month on our cable bill. After looking at some alternatives such as streaming devices and services for streaming we decided to make a change. We actually didn't watch much television anyway, mostly animal shows and old movies, so we took the plunge. We got rid of our home phone and cable and kept high-speed internet. Because of where we live we only have a few choices for internet service, but once the market opens up, we may consider making a change. Do not hesitate to shop for the best deal

The first thing we did was purchase a streaming device for about $40.00. You need a television with HDMI and ours fortunately did. If you buy another one for a second tv, it will be another $40. (we got ours on sale for $35) Then we subscribed to a few streaming services – all costing less than $10 each that gave us access to the latest movies and tv shows.

We pay under $30 for all of our streaming services and $83 a month for our internet access which is required to stream. Our total is still about $90 cheaper than what we use to pay for cable and we enjoy it a lot more. If you aren't interested in streaming tv shows or movies, you can save even more by going with a lower speed internet service provider.

There are certain strategies and marketing tactics used by cable companies. You need to have wisdom to deal with them. Do an online search of your cable company for complaints and you will probably find many problems.

When you look at your bill, you will see a list of fees and taxes added on each month. You should always ask for the bottom line of what cable will cost you monthly with all fees and taxes included before signing up for a service. That way you can avoid the shock of getting your first bill in the mail and seeing unexpected charges.

One charge that shocked me was to rent the modem and router for internet service. It does not matter what provider you use, almost all charge this rental fee. I recommend purchasing your own modem/router to eliminate the monthly cost. The price for a modem/router combo is usually less than $100.00. Contact your internet provider first to make sure any equipment you purchase is compatible. And as always, buy your new service in person if possible and shop around and do research before spending your money!

CONCLUSION

One of the principles of *Essential Practical Wisdom for Seniors* is that you must be empowered with knowledge when buying and spending. What are some of the things you should do before buying most products and services? The first thing to do is research what you can afford. Secondly, set a reasonable budget before shopping by deciding how much you can afford to spend and what you are willing to pay. This set amount will also help to keep you from buying more than you need.

A good rule to follow is: Money saved is money earned so watch the flow of your money. Use wisdom by seeking out and weighing good advice carefully. Join senior-focused organizations like AARP which only costs $16 a year and is well worth the investment. Being a member of organizations that serve older Americans provides you with additional benefits and discounts on a wide range of expenses

In the future, other *Essential Practical Wisdom* guides will offer some more in-depth information on many other topics, including:

- Relationships

- Technology

- Social Media

- Car Buying

- Insurance Buying

- Jobs

- Retirement

- Spirituality

I hope this book has enriched you and that you join me and my husband J. Edward Collier on this journey of embracing *Essential Practical Wisdom* in all aspects of your life.

Visit www.essentialpracticalwisdom.com to join the mailing list and get the inside scoop on when future books are released.

ABOUT THE AUTHOR

Lin Collier is a wife, mother, grandmother, great grandmother and a person dedicated to empowering older people with essential practical wisdom. As someone who is enjoying life as a wise and empowered senior, Lin is the co-founder of Reilloc Publishing who is currently writing a novel and about to launch out into the blogging community.

ESSENTIAL PRACTICAL WISDOM

JIM COLLIER, PHD

COMING SOON

www.essentialpracticalwisdom.com